May happiness touch your life today as warmly as you have touched the lives of others.

••• Rebecca Forsythe

People who deal with life

generously and large-heartedly

go on multiplying relationships

to the end. ••• A. C. Benson

Those who
bring sunshine
to the lives of
others cannot
keep it from
themselves.

 J. M. Barrie

Ultimately, the best gifts are the ones given from the heart, gifts that infuse our rituals with feelings and values. They're the ones that bring joy to the recipient and the giver—joy to the world.

••• Frances Lefkowitz

Each of us will one day be judged

by our standard of life,

not by our standard of living;

by our measure of giving,

not by our measure of wealth;

by our simple goodness,

not by our seeming greatness.

••• William Arthur Ward

Always demanding the best of oneself,
living with honor, devoting one's talents
and gifts to the benefits of others—
these are the measures of success
that endure when material things
have passed away.

••• Gerald R. Ford

The only thing you take
with you when you're gone
is what you leave behind.

••• John Allston

Most of us would like to end our
lives feeling both that we had a
good time and that we left the world
a little better than we found it.

••• Philip Slater

I expect to pass through this world but once.

Any good thing, therefore, that I can do

or any kindness I can show to any fellow creature,

let me do it now.

Let me not defer nor neglect it,

for I shall not pass this way again. ••• Stephen Grellet

A great life is the sum total of all the worthwhile things you've been doing one by one. ... Richard Bach

Nearly every problem our world faces is currently being solved in some community by some group or some individual. Imagine what might happen if we could only get all these good hearts and minds connected so that we could collectively tackle our problems.

••• Diane Branson

Every person is responsible for all the good within the scope of his abilities, and for no more, and none can tell whose sphere is the largest.

••• Gail Hamilton

There is in each of us
so much goodness
that if we could see
its glow, it would
light the world.

··· Sam Friend

We won't always know whose lives we touched and made better for our having cared, because actions can sometimes have unforeseen ramifications. What's important is that you do care and you act. ••• Charlotte Lunsford

The accumulation of small, optimistic acts produces quality in our culture and in your life. Our community resonates in tense times to individual acts of grace.

··· Jennifer James

It is time for greatness—not for greed. It's a time for idealism—not ideology. It is a time not just for compassionate words, but compassionate action.

••• Marian Wright Edelman

If the world is to be healed through human efforts, I am convinced it will be by ordinary people, people whose love for this life is even greater than their fear. ••• Joanna Macy

Give a smile to someone passing,
Thereby making his morning glad;
It may greet you in the evening
When your own heart may be sad.

··· Unknown

Drop a pebble in the water

And its ripples reach out far;

And the sunbeams dancing on them

May reflect them to a star.

We cannot live only for ourselves. A thousand fibers connect us with our fellowmen; and along those fibers, as sympathetic threads, our actions run as causes, and they come back to us as effects. •••• Herman Melville

The noblest question in the world is,
"What good may I do in it?"

••• Benjamin Franklin

The luxury
of doing good
surpasses every
other personal
enjoyment.

··· John Gay

Time has a wonderful
way of showing us
what really matters.

••• Margaret Peters

The work of your heart, the work of

taking time, to listen, to help, is also

your gift to the whole of the world.

••• Jack Kornfield

Your presence is
a present to the world.

••• Unknown

There is no tally sheet in the
exchange of small kindnesses;
but there is shared memory
and, from each person,
the assurance of good
things to come.

••• Lady Borton

He who wishes to secure the good of others has already secured his own.

••• Confucius

Really big people are,
above everything else,
courteous, considerate
and generous—not just
to some people in some
circumstances—but to
everyone all the time.

••• Thomas J. Watson, Jr.

Thank you to all the people
in the world who are
always ten percent kinder
than they need to be.

That's what really makes
the world go 'round.

••• Helen Exley

Having a big heart has nothing to do with how big your bank account is. Everyone has something to give. Some people give time, some money, some their skills and connections, some literally give their life's blood...but everyone has something to give. ··· Barbara Bush

Heart, instinct, principles.

People should know what you stand for
and what you won't. ··· Unknown

Goodness is the only

investment that never fails.

••• Henry David Thoreau

Being a good human being is good business.

••• Paul Hawken

it was someone who sought no recognition,
but the impact of their character and kindness
in our lives was heroic.

••• Stephen M. Wolf

Each of us can look back upon someone who made a great difference in our lives, often a teacher whose wisdom or simple acts of caring made an impression. In all likelihood,

The person we all love and appreciate is the one who's coming in the door when everybody else is going out. ••• Mason Cooley

We can always depend on
some people to make the best,
instead of the worst,
of whatever happens.

••• Sandra Wilde

The pieces I am,
she gathers them and
gives them back to me
in all the right order.

••• Toni Morrison

There are people who
take the heart out of you,
and there are people
who put it back.

... Elizabeth David

When we seek for connection, we restore the world to wholeness.

Our seemingly separate lives become meaningful as we discover

how truly necessary we are to each other. ••• Margaret Wheatley

All life connects.
Nothing happens that is meaningless.

··· Kobi Yamada

He that can give to his city any blessing, he who can be a good citizen while he lives here, he that can make better homes, he that can be a blessing whether he works in the shop or sits behind the counter or keeps house, whatever be his life, he who would be great anywhere must first be great in his own Philadelphia.

••• Russell Herman Conwell

Nothing that I can do will change the structure of the universe. But maybe, by raising my voice I can help the greatest of all causes—goodwill among men and peace on earth. ••• Albert Einstein

You are one individual on a small planet in a little solar system in one of the far-flung galaxies... but you can still make a difference. ··· Unknown

Nothing is more beautiful or powerful than an individual acting out of his or her conscience, thus helping to bring the collective conscience to life.

••• Norman Cousins

It takes courage for a person
to listen to their own goodness
and act on it.

··· Pablo Casals

Few of us will do the spectacular deeds of heroism that spread themselves across the pages of our newspapers in big black headlines.

But we can all be heroic in the little things of everyday life. We can do the helpful things, say the kind words, meet the difficulties with courage and high hearts, stand up for the right when the cost is high, keep our word even though it means sacrifice, be a giver instead of a destroyer. Often this quiet, humble heroism is the greatest heroism of all. ··· Wilfred Peterson

Do your little bit of
good where you are;
it's those little bits of
good put together that
overwhelm the world.

··· Archbishop Desmond Tutu

When the world seems large and complex,
we need to remember that great world ideals
all begin in some home neighborhood.

••• **Konrad Adenauer**

All of you reading these words have loved someone,

have done someone a kindness, have healed a wound,

have taken on a challenge, have created something

beautiful, and have enjoyed breathing the air of

existence. Every moment you make a difference.

••• "Random Acts of Kindness"

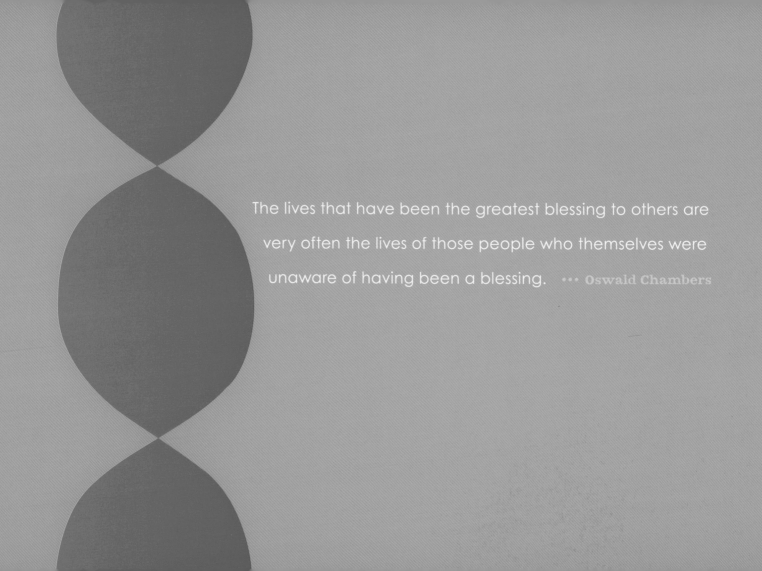

The lives that have been the greatest blessing to others are very often the lives of those people who themselves were unaware of having been a blessing. ••• Oswald Chambers

The good you do is not lost
though you forget it.

We all know special people who go about their daily lives, quietly and genuinely giving so much of themselves, but expecting so little in return. If only they realized what a difference they make in the world. ••• Dan Zadra

If you have a great friend or acquaintance,
take the time to let them know that they are great.

••• Jeri Bidel

Celebrating the Difference You Make

Pick a flower on earth and you move the farthest star. ··· **Paul Dirac**

The simplest questions are always the most profound. Does one person matter? Can anyone really change things for the better? Will the countless little things you do today—listening, caring, reaching out—actually make a difference?

The truth is, there are no little things. Everything is connected. We don't always get to see whose lives we touched and made better for our having cared. But we do know that every act of kindness, contribution or example quietly touches one heart, that in turn touches another, rippling out in ways we may never see. "The effect of one good-hearted person is incalculable," wrote Óscar Arias. This book celebrates the difference you make, not just to those who know you best, but to the world around you.

ACKNOWLEDGEMENTS

These quotations were gathered lovingly but unscientifically over several years and/or were contributed by many friends or acquaintances. Some arrived—and survived in our files—on scraps of paper and may therefore be imperfectly worded or attributed. To the authors, contributors and original sources, our thanks, and where appropriate, our apologies. –The Editors

WITH SPECIAL THANKS TO

Jason Aldrich, Gerry Baird, Jay Baird, Neil Beaton, Josie Bissett, Laura Boro, M.H. Clark, Jim and Alyssa Darragh & Family, Rob Estes, Michael and Leianne Flynn & Family, Sarah Forster, Michael Hedge, Liz Heinlein, Renee Holmes, Jennifer Hurwitz, Heidi Jones, Carol Anne Kennedy, June Martin, Jessica Phoenix and Tom DesLongchamp, Steve and Janet Potter & Family, Heidi & José Rodriguez, Diane Roger, Alie Satterlee, Kirsten and Garrett Sessions, Andrea Shirley, Heidi Yamada & Family, Justi and Tote Yamada & Family, Bob and Val Yamada, Kaz and Kristin Yamada & Family, Tai and Joy Yamada, Anne Zadra, August and Arline Zadra, and Gus and Rosie Zadra.

CREDITS

Compiled by Dan Zadra
Designed by Sarah Forster
Edited by Kristel Wills

ISBN: 978-1-932319-62-0

2nd Printing. 06 10   Printed in China

GOOD

PERSON

COMPENDIUM™
INCORPORATED

live inspired.

••• Compiled by Dan Zadra ••• Designed by Sarah Forster ••• Edited by Kristel Wills •••